GOD MADE KITTENS

Written by Marian Bennett

Illustrated by Kathryn Marlin

ISBN 978-1-4964-0319-3

Printed in China

21	20	19	18	17	16	1
7	6	5	4	3	2	1

Tyndale House Publishers, Inc.
Carol Stream, Illinois

When God made kittens, he
must have laughed
to see them run.

He made them to pounce, jump, and roll, and have all kinds of fun!

God made kittens
with warm, soft fur,

bright shining eyes,
and a deep, deep purr.

They have sharp teeth and
tongues that feel like sand.

When a kitten licks you,
it tickles your hand.

Kittens come in many colors—
brown and black and tan and white

Some have stripes, and some have spots. They are such a silly sight!

Kittens' tails may be large, or they may be small.

God made
the Manx
to have no
tail at all.

Curious kittens like to explore with glee.

They can hide in a box

or even
up a tree.

Kittens like warm milk and soft beds, and someone to pet them and scratch their heads.

God made kittens as cute as can be—to bring happiness and love to you and to me!

Let's Talk about It

1. Who made kittens?

2. What colors do kittens come in?

3. What sounds do kittens make?

4. What do kittens like?

5. Why did God make kittens?

Matching Items

fish

mouse

cat

butterfly

Word Search

```
R  D  K  C  S  P  Z  Z
Y  R  W  I  U  L  Z  C
F  J  U  N  T  T  X  W
K  Q  Z  P  Q  T  E  K
M  I  L  K  Z  E  E  L
X  V  M  Z  G  M  Y  N
P  L  S  Z  S  V  R  W
Z  O  B  M  H  M  F  L
```

Find these words

KITTEN • CUTE • PURR • MILK

Craft Activity

Make your own kitten mask!

Things you will need:
- large paper bag
- markers
- construction paper
- scissors
- glue

What to do:

1. Cut a large circle and two small triangles out of construction paper. These will be the face and ears of your kitten.

2. Open the paper bag and turn it upside down.

3. Glue the circle to one side of the bag.

4. Ask an adult to help you cut holes where the eyes should be. It helps to try on the bag first, mark the places where your eyes will look out, and then take off the bag and cut the holes.

5. Decorate the head with a cat's nose and mouth. Don't forget to draw whiskers!

6. Glue the triangles where the ears should be.

7. Have fun being a kitten!

COLORING PAGE

COLORING PAGE

Shape a lifestyle of faith expression in your child

— Our passion is to provide a creative outlet for kids to express their faith in a fun and meaningful way. Cultivate a deeper connection as you teach your child about the impact of God's love, building a legacy of relationship, creativity, and faith to last a lifetime.

Using interactive games, puzzles, and other activities, **Faith That Sticks resources** are a great go-to place for parents who want to teach their kids to love God and to know how much he loves them!

learn more at faiththatsticks.com

More about Reading Levels

PRE-READERS

Books appropriate for pre-readers have
- pictures that reinforce the text
- simple words
- short, simple sentences
- repetition of words and patterns
- large print

BEGINNING READERS

Books appropriate for beginning readers have
- pictures that reinforce the text
- intermediate words
- longer sentences
- simple stories
- dialogue between story characters

INDEPENDENT READERS

Books appropriate for independent readers have
- less need for pictorial support with the text
- more advanced vocabulary
- paragraphs
- longer stories
- more complex subjects

"There are perhaps no days of our childhood we lived so fully as those we spent with a favorite book." — MARCEL PROUST